G.U.I.D.E

Differentiated Instruction for Christian Educators

by Dr. Beth Ackerman

LIBERTY
UNIVERSITY.

Press
Lynchburg, VA
www.liberty.edu/libertyuniversitypress

Liberty University Press
1971 University Blvd.
Lynchburg, VA 24502

www.liberty.edu/libertyuniversitypress

Scripture quotations are taken from the *Holy Bible, New International Version*®. *NIV*®.
Copyright © 1973, 1978, 1984 by International Bible Society. All rights reserved.

Ackerman, Beth.
Guide to Differentiated Instruction for Christian Educators / Beth Ackerman – 1st ed.
ISBN 978-1-935986-26-3
1. Students — Psychology. 2. Teaching.
3. Differentiated Education. 4. Christian Education.
I. Title

First edition, April 2012

10 9 8 7 6 5 4 3 2 1

Printed in the United States of America

Publisher's Acknowledgments

A special thank you to all the individuals who assisted in the creation of this publication:

Proofreader: Rebecca Murtha
Editorial Assistant: Alicia Whitecavage
Project Editor: Leo Percer
Editorial Manager: Sarah Funderburke
Layout and Graphics: Coreen Montagna and Shannon Tarvin
Special Help: Arielle Bielicki

#807986256

Table of Contents

What is Differentiated Instruction?

Differentiated instruction is a new way of thinking and teaching in which the teacher adapts learning to the student.[1] Learning is no longer based on the teacher or the textbook or the curriculum; it is based on the student. 1 Corinthians 9:19-23 states, "I have become all things to all men" (paraphrase). That is what we have to do as teachers. If a teacher has a student (let's call her *Suzie*) who is visual, then the teacher needs to become visual. If Suzie is a leader, the teacher needs to teach her and show her how to become a better leader. If she is a kinesthetic learner, then the teacher has to become kinesthetic as well. Thus, a classroom teacher becomes all things to all students. This is differentiated instruction in practice. As Christians, differentiated instruction includes teaching and reaching out to students with varying abilities. This is based on your students, their profiles, their modalities, their interests, what matters most to them. They become equal in the planning process!

---

1. Tomlinson, C. A., (2001). *How to differentiate instruction in mixed-ability classrooms (2nd Ed)*. Alexandria, VA: ASCD.

Great Commission

Our Mission in Reaching *ALL* Students

This book is intended to be a call to all Christian educators to reach all children and adolescents in our Christian and public schools. As Christian educators, we want the world to see God's grace and glory through our students. This can be done as teachers guide students to success through understanding their varying gifts. The Body of Christ can function completely only once we are able to include these often hidden treasures and gifts in our churches and schools. Guiding students in their varying abilities will better equip them to impact our world for Christ.

Scripture is clear on many things. All Christian denominations tend to agree that the *Great Commission* calls for us to reach ALL people. We are not to reach out to only those who fit into our "boxes" and "perceptions" of who might make good Christians or who might learn information differently or struggle to grasp information. Our commission is to reach *all* people. How does this apply to those learners from different levels? How do we help those who do not fit the "mold" and fit into a Christian school? Should our Christian schools help in fulfilling the Great Commission to reaching *all* people? As Christian schools, should we take these "different" or sometimes struggling students? According to Scripture, the answer is clearly that we need to reach *all* people, to include the diverse and struggling learners in our Christian schools, and to do all we can to help them be successful.

Being Elite and Serving ALL Students

Christian schools have to concern themselves with the idea of being the best; creating schools that stand above all other schools and demonstrate excellence in their craft of education. When trying to meet these standards, schools often find themselves trying to decide whether they should be elite and among the best *or* whether they should care for "the least of these" and reach *all* students. All too often, Christian school administrators describe the success of their schools by the entrance exams, students' scores on various achievement tests, how many of their students go to elite colleges, or how many even go to college at all. While these are great measures of success, there are other components of elite schools. While parents and school boards like to hear and tout these numbers, all Christian schools must ask themselves a very difficult question: Is this a private school, or is this a Christian school?

As Christians we need to evaluate what Scripture says about reaching all students. A great passage that addresses which population should be welcomed in our Christian schools is Luke 14:12-14. Jesus says, "When you give a luncheon or dinner, do not invite your friends, your brothers or sisters, your relatives, or your rich neighbors; if you do, they may invite you back and so you will be repaid. But when you give a banquet, invite the poor, the crippled, the lame, the blind, and you will be blessed. Although they cannot repay you, you will be repaid at the resurrection of the righteous." Many of our Christian schools are built from "friends, brothers, relatives, rich neighbors, etc." However, we should be concerned about "the poor, the crippled, the lame, the blind." We need to be concerned for those who are struggling—the least of these. This is what is righteous. Job 29:14-16 also shows this righteousness as Job shares, "I put on righteousness as my clothing; justice was my robe and my turban. I was eyes to the blind and feet to the lame. I was a father to the needy; I took up the case of the stranger." Job paints a picture of accepting and caring for "the least of these." In Christian schools we can address this by differentiating instruction for our diverse learners. Think of how much more powerful Christian schools and educators could be if we had diverse learners in our schools, which we then empowered to go out and reach the world for Christ. Differentiated instruction is biblical and is something that we all should be doing.

Champions for Christ

One thing that concerns Christian schools is their ability to train students to be disciples for Christ. In order to teach our students how to interact with a diverse population, we need to include diverse students in our schools. If we concern ourselves with having only elite students in our schools, then we often create a sheltered environment for these students. While administrators may be tempted to protect students by keeping them away from the struggles of the world, if they are not around diverse people in school then they may be ill-equipped to be disciples for Christ in the world.

Perhaps the most compelling argument for including diverse students in Christian schools can be found in studying all the great characters, prophets, and disciples in the Bible. These historical figures rarely represented the elite, and every one of them had a broken human element that God used to show His greatness. There was Moses, who was not eloquent, but God gave him a voice, and Paul who persecuted Christians, but God changed his heart. God doesn't use only His elite children, He uses *all* His children.

All too often schools have tight entrance standards to limit the population (both in size and in ability), but there is a danger in these entrance standards. The teacher may not feel responsible for the final product, the student. If the student comes to the teacher already refined and molded, then where is the true joy in teaching and discovering the beauty of that student? However when a teacher is blessed with a struggling student, then the teacher becomes responsible for the product. This can be a problem for teachers in that it can cause much anxiety. Teachers easily fall prey to this anxiety because they feel their jobs are judged much more closely if their schools accept struggling students. Administrators and parents are a very important part of this philosophy, as the success of a teacher is no longer *only* determined by performance standards. While performance standards are important and do deserve a place in our schools, teachers are working with diverse and struggling learners whose measures of success can be greater than those shown on a test.

Working with diverse and struggling learners is a challenge. The rest of the previously mentioned passage in Luke 14:12-14 says, "you will not be repaid until the resurrection of the righteous" (paraphrase). You will not feel repaid by the world's standards for working with difficult and challenging students, but by knowing you are doing what is right and good, you can experience God's peace and the Fruit of the Spirit. Teachers should work very hard in order to help all students be successful, and they must challenge their own thinking about the different learner. Teachers should spend time discovering the great characters of the Bible who were indeed "the least of these," seeing that these great characters remind us of the students who challenge teachers the most. Teachers have to believe that *all* students deserve a chance at success in our classrooms, regardless of the students' backgrounds, learning styles, and/or disabilities. These students not only deserve a chance in a Christian school to be taught biblical truths, but also need these truths to help them in their personal struggle more than any other student does. Until teachers, administrators, and parents really believe this truth, there is nothing else this book can do to help. Otherwise, excuses are created on why this won't work in "*our* classrooms" or with "*this* student." Christian educators need to embrace this idea and believe it is necessary to the cause of Christian education.

There are a variety of reasons schools do not feel equipped to take the "different" or "struggling" learner. One of the biggest reasons is that teachers and administrators do not feel that they are equipped to deal with these students in their classrooms. This book is specifically written to give administrators and teachers the tools to feel they are adequately prepared to teach all students and children. It is intended to be a quick and simple read that gives educators the tried and true techniques that are successfully being implemented in diverse classrooms all over the world.

<u>U</u>nderstanding Differentiation

The Learners

Many lesson-planning experts believe in the idea of differentiating instruction for our diverse learners. One of the founders of the essential elements to a lesson plan stated that expecting children in the same age group to all successfully learn from the exact same materials is akin to expecting the same children to all wear the same size clothing. Differentiated instruction is not anything new in our field. This is not rocket science; it's really just a new, pretty name for something the experts always said we should do.

All teachers at some point in their career, or perhaps every year in their career, have that student who really challenges them—a student who can't organize; who doesn't know how to follow directions; who can't stay on task and attentive to his/her work; who has trouble interpreting and remembering information; who can't do basic skills; who has low expectations from others; and/or who has difficulty learning, using meta-cognition, and making connections. In addition these students have learning styles different from the teachers'. This is the student who challenges teachers the most. What do we do with this student? The chart below is a list teachers may use to describe a child who is struggling in school:

• Poor organization	• Has low expectations by others
• Problems following directions	• Doesn't appear to know how to learn
• Not staying on task and attending	• Unable to make connections
• Unable to interpret & remember information	• Demonstrates learning styles that are different than the teacher's
• Behind in basic skills	• Is not an active learner

A learning disability is actually a scattering of abilities across a variety of measures. Students are typically diagnosed with a learning disability in one or more specific areas. Students could possibly even be in the high or gifted range of ability but score low in one psychological subtest and be diagnosed with a learning disability. Teachers may often feel that these students are lazy when they do not seem to achieve in their ability range because their abilities may be affected in just one area. For example, a student may struggle with spelling while being very good at learning facts. Part of understanding differentiated instruction is recognizing that students can have strengths across subjects while also having different interests, styles of learning, etc.

In addition to these issues, we also have the varying learning modalities: visual, auditory, and kinesthetic.[2] What is important to recognize is that the child who does not have the same modality as the teacher is the one who will be the most difficult for that teacher to teach. There has been a lot of research conducted in this area of modalities, but there are so many other unique issues surrounding our students, such as Gardner's Theories of Multiple Intelligences.[3] Gardner included a broad spectrum of learners with strengths in visual (spatial), bodily (kinesthetic), musical, interpersonal, intrapersonal, and linguistic intelligences. Thus, educators must ask themselves what to do with so many different levels, types of learners, and learner interests. The answer is quite simple—*differentiated instruction.*

Many educators do not realize that differentiated instruction is not a new concept. It actually is not even rooted in helping the struggling learner. The roots of differentiated instruction are in gifted education.[4] However, teachers and researchers quickly realized that these same techniques that have been effective for the gifted learner are effective for *all* learners.

---

2. Dunn, R., & Dunn, K. J. (1978). *Teaching students through their individual learning styles.* Englewood Cliffs, NJ: Prentice-Hall.

3. Gardner, H. (1999) *Intelligence Reframed. Multiple intelligences for the 21st century,* New York: Basic Books, p 292.

4. Tomlinson, C. A., (2001). *How to differentiate instruction in mixed-ability classrooms (2nd Ed).* Alexandria, VA: ASCD.

What is the answer?	
• "I wish there was something I could do…but…" • "I have too many students…" • "I do not have time…" • "What about everyone else in the class?"	Differentiated Instruction Utilizing Learning Strategies

Key Principles for a Differentiated Classroom

What Matters In Subject Matter

First of all, teachers have to determine what matters in the subject matter.[5] Teachers have to begin their planning by asking themselves what content students need to know and why. This is the very first step to differentiated instruction. What is the key objective that we wish the students to know? Why? Is it something that will be covered on standardized assessments? What matters about what we are covering? What are we going to learn at the end of this unit? We obviously want to learn the objective, but more importantly, we want to know why that objective is important. Is it important because all the other fifth grade teachers are doing it? Is it important because a teacher's guide book to the student's textbook says to do it? Why is it important? This is the focus of a teacher who utilizes differentiated instruction. This process is a non-negotiable aspect of differentiated instruction.

Teachers often make two errors when considering content coverage. The first mistake you often find is a teacher may cover too many details in the subject matter while missing what is really important. On the other hand, differentiated instruction makes teaching and learning much more enjoyable. For example, there is so much you can do with teaching the eight planets. A teacher utilizing differentiated instruction might use mnemonics

---

5. Tomlinson, C. A., (2001). *How to differentiate instruction in mixed-ability classrooms (2nd Ed)*. Alexandria, VA: ASCD.

G
U
I
D
E

9

and/or Styrofoam balls to represent the planets. Many teachers would be surprised to learn that they are already incorporating some elements of differentiated instruction correctly. The second common error is that teachers have so much fun incorporating differentiated instruction into the classroom that the content gets lost. A fun powerful assignment is being completed such as a diorama of the eight planets. And while so much excitement is around the materials ,the visual appearance, and creativity, the content and specific learning objectives can be lost. The teacher has to utilize her content specific knowledge of the subject matter and learning objectives of the subject matter when she sits down and plans with her students. The teacher knows what is important and practical for her students' lives and furthering their education. What matters in the subject matter?

Our Varying Gifts
The Bible speaks strongly about our varying abilities. Christian educators should familiarize themselves with 1 Corinthians 12, Romans 12, and Ephesians 4. The truths found in these verses are also seen in current research. Gardner proposed that intelligence as we currently understand it does not sufficiently encompass the wide variety of abilities that humans actually display.[6] For example, a child who masters multiplication easily is not necessarily more intelligent than a child who is weak in math but stronger in another kind of intelligence (for instance, spelling). Gardner proposes that there many different types of intelligence. This table is a brief summary of Gardner's multiple intelligences.

---

6. Gardner, H. (2004) *Changing minds: The art and science of changing our own and other people's minds.* Boston: Harvard Business School Press, p. 196.

Gardner's Multiple Intelligences[7]

Intelligence	Description
Linguistic intelligence	Utilizing words effectively
Musical intelligence	Sensitive to sound and rhythm
Logical-Mathematical intelligence	Reasoning and calculating skills
Spatial intelligence	Acute awareness of environment
Bodily-Kinesthetic intelligence	Keen sense of body awareness and effectively using the body
Interpersonal intelligence	Understanding and interacting well with others
Intrapersonal intelligence	Understanding of personal goals and emotions

Christians would agree that "there are different kinds of gifts, but the same Spirit distributes them. There are different kinds of service, but the same Lord. There are different kinds of working, but in all of them and in everyone it is the same God at work." (1 Corinthians 12:4-6). The emphasis on "all" again sounds like the Great Commission. This concept applies to *all* of our students; they may have different gifts and abilities, but they are also *all* of equal importance.

Gardner's ideas continued to mirror how "God works in all of them" by stating that if a child learns multiplication at a different pace, then he or she may (a) best learn the given material through a different approach, (b) excel in a field outside of mathematics, or (c) even be looking at the multiplication process at a fundamentally deeper level, which can result in a seeming slowness that hides a mathematical intelligence that is potentially higher than that of a child who easily grasps the multiplication table.[8]

7. Gardner, H. (1999) *Intelligence Reframed. Multiple intelligences for the 21st century,* New York: Basic Books, p. 292

8. Gardner, H. (2004) *Changing minds: The art and science of changing our own and other people's minds.* Boston: Harvard Business School Press, p. 196.

Adjust Content, Process, and Product to Your Students

Here is the format for typical classroom instruction: Textbook, textbook, textbook, quiz. Textbook, textbook, textbook, test, and so on. There are a good percentage of students who learn this way (direct instruction); however, this will only work for the students whose learning profile matches this instructional style. Differentiated instruction does not discount direct instruction, but rather includes it as an effective teaching strategy.[9] Direct instruction is most effective for independent and auditory learners who learn through rote memory, but it is just one of many effective teaching tools. Textbooks are typically the main element in direct instruction. In differentiated instruction a teacher will still utilize the textbook; however, the teacher will adjust the *content* that that is being covered and the *process* in which it is being covered as well as the *product* that the student will produce.

Differentiated Content

Differentiated Instruction **=** Differentiated Process

Differentiated Product

Adjusting teaching methods in order to reach a broad spectrum of students is a big responsibility for teachers, but teachers must consider the fact that *all students are active participants in the learning process*. This is best done by adjusting the content, process, and product to the individual student profile. The teacher must become all things to all students, based off students' readiness, profile and interests. This part of differentiated instruction is depicted in 1 Corinthians 9:20-23, "To the Jews I became like a Jew, to win the Jews. To those under the law I became like one under the law (though I myself am not under the law), so as to win those under the law. To those not having the law I became like one not having the law (though I am not free from God's law but am under Christ's law), so as to win those not having the law. To the weak I became weak, to win the weak. I have become all things to all people so that by all possible means I might save some. I do all this for the sake of the gospel, that I may share in its blessings."

---

9. Swanson, H. L. (2001). "Research on interventions for adolescents with learning disabilities: A meta-analysis of outcomes related to higher-order processing." *Elementary School Journal*, 101, 331–348.

Goals of a Differentiated Classroom are Maximum Growth and Individual Success

As teachers we really are looking for individual praise, individual success, and individual reward, so how do we make the individual student feel successful? Matthew 23:4 speaks of the scribes and Pharisees and how "they tie up heavy, cumbersome loads and put them on other people's shoulders, but they themselves are not willing to lift a finger to move them." Teachers who expect a lot of their students should be willing to share in the "burden" of mastering the material that is presented. The Christian educator's goal should be to help students work through their burdens rather than to add to them. Taking the time to reach all students and help them succeed on an individual basis is hard work, but it is a "heavy load" that educators (especially Christian educators) should be willing to bear.

One of the major differences between special education and general education is that special educators have the privilege of working with individuals. Special educators write individualized education plans (IEPs) and adjust learning for Johnny, and for Susie, and for Karen. Conversely, general educators see a class of twenty-five students, and they all have to be successful, and they all have to do these exams, and they all have to move through the curriculum together. With differentiated instruction, the goal is to focus on individual success rather than just class percentages. Christian educators might liken this concept to the Luke 15 story of the lost sheep. The great shepherd leaves the flock to care for the one injured sheep. As Christian educators we need to bring our struggling students back to the fold and back to learning on a regular basis.

Administrative Support

Gone are the days of the rigid classroom environment where the students simply sit still and look at the teacher all day. Of course maintaining order in a classroom is still important, but a classroom should ultimately be a place that fosters creativity and activity. For this reason administrator involvement is very important. A school principal who is walking down the halls may look into the differentiated classroom and see what appears to be chaos. In a differentiated classroom things do not always have an appearance of being controlled, but if a teacher is effectively differentiating instruction, the teacher and the students both know what matters in the subject matter. When the principal walks by and hears all that noise, a teacher or student can clearly articulate the goals being covered: "We're doing the characteristics of the eight planets today." Other issues that will be covered later, such as effectively utilizing rubrics, will also help achieve administrative support for an active classroom.

Be Flexible

A teacher must be flexible in a differentiated classroom. Things will change, projects won't work, and the teacher will have to adapt. Psalm 131:1-2 says, "My heart is not proud, Lord, my eyes are not haughty; I do not concern myself with great matters or things too wonderful for me. But, I have calmed and quieted myself [...] like a weaned child I am content." This verse demonstrates the rest and calm a teacher should have when relinquishing the appearance of control.

Emphasize Critical and Creative Thinking

The fun of differentiated instruction is that a teacher begins to see students thinking on their own. As Proverbs 14:15 says, "The simple believe anything, but the prudent give thoughts to their steps." The reason differentiated instruction originated in gifted education is because of those students' abilities to be able to think creatively and critically. Teachers often are stuck trying to determine how to cover the content. Then students are not taught to think ahead and are more concerned about memorizing content to pass a test rather than giving critical thought to the content and what is being learned. Here is a quick look at a typical classroom:

> The teacher is greeting his/her students at the door as they come into class. Students come into the room and have an activity on their desks to engage them for a few minutes. The teacher then moves to the front of the class to begin the teaching (or lecture). Let's say this is a math class, so the teacher is doing some direct instruction. "Okay, put away your warm up activity, and let's get started with the lesson," the teacher says. The students work through the notes and the book together, do some problems together, and then they begin to practice on their own. "Begin your worksheet and independent practice," says the teacher. Here comes the dreaded moment. In ten seconds Johnny is

hollering, "I'm already done." Truthfully, he was done before the teacher even said, "Get out your workbook," because this bright student knows the routine and knows what the teacher was going to say. The teacher has ten students who are working and appear to "get it" and then there are six or seven students who are saying, "What? Huh? What book? I brought the wrong book. I need a pencil." This is the typical classroom.

What did the teacher do to teach Johnny critical and creative thinking skills? What do we do about those six or seven students who are taking all of our time? How does the teacher fix the fact that these ten average students seem to be teaching themselves? Once again, one answer to all of these questions is differentiated instruction. A quick solution with a low level of preparation would be to make Johnny the tutor for the other six or seven students, encouraging him to go around and help them. Now, some teachers might see that as a "cop-out," so a teacher utilizing peer tutoring like this would have to make sure the right goals were behind this strategy. Often, these really gifted kids know the answer; they just do not know the process. Knowing the process is equally important, so providing Johnny with the opportunity to go and explain it is fostering critical thinking. However, it has to be done with that goal in mind. It can't be done because, as a teacher, "I'm tired and do not feel like working with any students today, so Johnny is my assistant teacher even though we're not paying him anything." It has to be done with the right attitude, but peer tutoring, which is strongly validated by research, is an example of differentiated instruction.[10] We've talked about teaching critical thinking, but what about teaching *creative* thinking? This is another situation for Johnny: "Johnny, flip your paper over, I want you to make two extra problems that we will use for warm-ups tomorrow." Creating a problem is a higher order of thinking skill than simply solving a problem. These are just a few small examples of what differentiated instruction looks like at a low level of preparation and what many teachers may already be doing.

10. Stenhoff, D. M., & Lignugarisk/Kraft, B. (2007). "A review of the effects of peer tutoring on students with mild disabilities in secondary settings." *Exceptional Children*, 74(1), 8–30.

Other ideas for increasing creativity in English can be finding various and creative ways to play with words. Have students use magnetic poetry to show them how much fun it is to put words together in different ways. Mad-libs are another fun way to play with words and allow creativity. Mad-libs are word games where students give a list of words based on the description of the word (such as adverb, adjective, passive verb, etc.). Then these words are placed into a fill-in-the-blank story. When the completed story is read, it is usually very silly and often involves situations and objects that readers wouldn't normally expect. Retelling Aesop stories using people instead of animals can also be a fun activity. These are just a few ideas for one content area, and there are many more exciting ideas that can be found on the Internet.

Be Engaging

Students need to be engaged in the learning process. This can be challenging as many teachers go into the field because of a perception that they will have autonomy in their classroom. Sometimes teachers have a hard time understanding that they must collaborate with students in learning together. Here is a wonderful example of what this type of collaboration can look like:

> A teacher was working with her students on a unit on budget planning. All of her students were planning a family vacation and determining the budget for the vacation. She was having difficulty with Johnny, a student who was refusing to participate and causing behavior problems in the class. The teacher was so frustrated with Johnny because, while the rest of the class was having a lot of fun with the unit, he was constantly disrupting instruction. Later, the teacher realized that a key component to the lesson was missing. She didn't collaborate with the students prior to planning this unit and activity. She realized this when one of her colleagues asked her, "Would Johnny ever actually *go* on a family vacation?" She said, "Oh. Probably not." The teacher then had the idea to ask Johnny if he had any other ideas for creating a budget (*remember—what matters in the subject matter*). Creating a budget was this teacher's goal. The textbook

offered cute ways of doing it, such as the family trip, but simply creating a budget was the real goal, so, she sat down with Johnny and said to him, "You have to set up a budget; that is our goal. Is there something besides a vacation that you would like to buy or do? Let's talk about a budget." In the end, Johnny came up with the idea of modifying a car and dressing it up. This was his plan, and sure enough it worked because he was a part of the collaborating; he was in the process. This is a picture of what student collaboration in unit planning would look like.

This is considered differentiated instruction because the teacher is looking at individual student interests, readiness, and profiles.

Instruction and Assessment Must Match

Matching instruction to assessment is the most important aspect of differentiated instruction. In a typical class, we simply cover material over and over until we give a test. Many teachers are now trying to differentiate their instruction. They differentiate instruction with really beautiful, fun activities. Perhaps they create shadow plays or have a science fair. The students and teachers might collaborate on some type of really big, powerful product (an approach to be discussed later in this book), but then the teacher follows up this powerful product with a paper and pencil test. This can be very frustrating for the student. With differentiated instruction, the difference is that instruction and assessment are always the same thing. Matching instruction and assessment goes back to basic lesson planning with formative and summative assessments.

Often teachers are preparing students for various state or achievement tests, so there are times where having a paper/pencil test is important for this preparation. However, life and most jobs typically consist of a series of projects or ideas to think through that involve some decision-making. After graduation, rarely is a paper/pencil test given to determine the success of an individual. The actual projects are analyzed to determine their success. That is why the instruction and the assessment are inseparable in differentiated instruction. This is done by utilizing rubrics and grading checklists. In some classrooms you often find exciting differentiated techniques and projects being done for the instruction part of the curriculum. But then they close the learning unit with a traditional test. Our active learners will score poorly on these paper and pencil assessments, not only because of the lack of activity during the testing time, but because no instruction was done for preparation of this type of assessment. If the instruction was completing a project, or reading a differentiated text, then the assessment should be on the completion of the project or on that differentiated text.

This is also done by recognizing the role of formative and summative evaluation as it relates to differentiated instruction. Formative evaluation is continuous throughout the learning process. It collects the learners profile, interests and readiness. But in addition it checks on the learner's prior knowledge of a subject as well as the learning process. Summative evaluation then checks the mastery of the subject, topic and/or skill of the learner. And all of this is done in the context of considering instruction and assessment.

Learning in Differential Instruction

Description of Strategy

Another important component of matching instruction and assessment is the need to scaffold assignments in order to get to the final product. Scaffolding is done by breaking learning down into smaller parts or steps.[11] Let's go back to the example of creating a budget. How do we get to that final project? What does the final project look like? How are students going to present it? Will it be a PowerPoint presentation? Are they going to practice doing a budget hearing? Is it going to be a family planning exercise, where students pretend to be different family members? What is that final project, and what is the process of completing it? English teachers have already mastered the concepts of scaffolding assignments. Often, the big paper for a high school English class is broken down into different parts. What is the first thing you have to come up with, and when is it due? For the high school English paper, the process looks something like this: topic, thesis, outline, note-cards, draft, revised draft, and the final copy. These are tiered assignments. Similarly, in differentiated instruction, the teacher is breaking down all of the major projects and assignments into steps.

---

11. Vygotsky, L.S. (1978). *Mind in Society*. Cambridge, MA: Harvard University Press.

One way in which teachers can collaborate with their students in differentiated instruction is to have students help determine the steps in the assignment. For example, if the class is going to do a budget, what do the students need? How much do the students have to spend? What kind of research do the students need to conduct? How are the teacher and students going to present the information? Then each of these parts of the assignments is turned in on a timeline. The teacher is breaking the assignments down and allowing the students to assist in the process, which increases critical thinking and adds to the collaborative process.

Create Learning Contracts

Ultimately, after a teacher has decided which steps need to be taken in the scaffolding process, the teacher and student will create a learning contract. Learning contracts often take the form of a rubric. There are some great online resources that will assist teachers and/or students in creating a grading rubric, and many of them are free. Below is an example of the components of a rubric for an English paper. A rubric is much more than just a list of what students need to do to get an "A." It is much more objective in that it also shows the student what a "C" project would look like in comparison to an "A" project or a failing project.

The example below shows how a rubric can be developed with criteria for grading and content.

Element	Excellent	Proficient	Developing
Thesis Statement	Original, well thought out	Good - not as engaging or original as "A" work	Confusing, poorly thought out
Development	Develops thesis in engaging manner	Good development of thesis	No evidence of maturity or persuasiveness
Support	Substantial support for thesis	Good support for thesis but not as substantial as "A" work	Little support for thesis - what's there is irrelevant or poorly incorporated

Alternative Assessments

If a teacher is differentiating instruction correctly, all of the assessments will be alternative assessments. This is where teachers are going to get into using rubrics to assess their students. Paper/pencil tests will now be used sparingly. Rubrics are key here. How do you assess a speech? What does a good speech look like? If there is no rubric to let the students see exactly what a good speech looks like, then an "A" speech has become arbitrary. University accreditation standards now require rubrics for all major assignments and achievement tests. Essays are also graded utilizing rubrics. Effectively utilizing rubrics has become a growing trend in education.

Delivery Methods

Differentiated instruction can be a challenge and can require a lot of preparation time and resources for a teacher and school; however, there are some quick and easy ways a teacher can differentiate instruction. This section will focus on these simple ideas and provide a list of examples. Many of these are self-explanatory, and others require more explanation. A teacher could look up any and all of them online for more ideas on how they can be utilized in the classroom.

Low Preparation Differentiation[12]

- Choices of Books and Materials
- Homework Options
- Reading Buddies
- Varied Journal Prompts
- Varied Pacing
- Student-Teacher Goal Setting
- Work Alone/Together
- Jigsaw
- Open-Ended Activities
- Flexible Seating
- Varied Computer Programs
- Varied Modes of Expression
- Varied Note Taking
- Varying Graphic Organizers
- Think-Pair-Share
- Collaboration, Independence, Cooperation

G U I D E

12. Pauk, H. (2001). *How to Study in College 7th Ed.* Houghton Mifflin Company.

Choices of Books and Materials

Letting students choose their books and materials is an easy way to incorporate differentiated instruction with little preparation required by the teacher. Instead of saying, "Everybody, tonight for homework you have to read pages thirteen through forty-two and then answer questions," tell the students that they have to read something about reptiles. The students can figure out if they want to do something on the Internet, from the library, or from the textbook. Students will often pick challenging material, or they will at least pick material they understand. Then the teacher will have to decide what the finished product is. What do the students have to submit to be sure that they did the assignment and that it was at their level of reading and understanding?

Homework Options

One of the hardest things about having students with learning disabilities is the issue of fairness. A good way to deal with this issue is differentiated instruction. This way everybody has alternatives. No longer does the teacher say, "Poor Johnny can't take notes by himself," or "Johnny will only get five spelling words instead of fifteen words." Not only is this unfair to the rest of the class who has the fifteen spelling words, but now the other students know that Johnny must be "slower" than them because he has been assigned less words. One way to address this issue is to have varied homework assignments. Actually, spelling is one of the places that teachers often already do this. Students can write definitions, write sentences, write the word three times; the student decides which assignment to complete. This works in spelling, but what about other subject areas? In math, for example, the student can choose two word problems or ten product problems. We will talk later in the High Preparation Differentiation section about how a teacher can use a Tic-Tac-Toe method to be sure that students are picking a variety of levels, difficulty, presentations, etc.

Varied Journal Prompts

Journal activities are a great way many teachers start class. However, providing varied journal prompts and journal options is a way to differentiate this activity. A teacher can do an online search of varied journal prompts and see many creative ideas for journal activities.

Open-Ended Activities

Open-ended activities are the really fun assignments. Teachers may have to put in a great deal of planning to come up with open-ended activities. However, students often find them to be most enjoyable, and they will last longer and get more mileage than a worksheet that can be done in three minutes. Thus, the effort of planning for differentiation pays off over planning a lot of small assignments that do not have the lasting effect of an open-ended assignment. A quick example of this would be to use old magazines for students to glue pictures of adjectives on a paper. Students enjoy this much more than a worksheet, and it has much more student buy-in.

Varied Modes of Expression

This is a big one in differentiated instruction. What are different ways that we can present information? Some people are gifted writers and some are gifted speakers. What are their options? How about music? Can they create a rap instead of a poem? Can they perform the rap? Can they write a play? Can they create a brochure or create a PowerPoint? Can they design a poster? There are so many different ways students can express their work that not only communicate in their learning style, but also allow them to use the gifts and talents God has given to them.

Varied Note Taking

A whole guidebook on differentiated instruction can be done on note taking alone. There are some teacher resource guides out there in which every unit offers a different way of taking notes. This is very important, because it is good college-preparation to learn how to take notes in a meaningful way. Instead of saying, "here are the notes" or "take this down this way," the teacher allows students to choose what works for them by practicing different methods. Fill-in-the-blank notes are classic (also called cloze notes). This is a great strategy to encourage students to follow along with the teacher's notes and lecture. Venn Diagrams (i.e., overlapping circles) are probably very familiar for comparing and contrasting topics. The Cornell method is used most commonly with struggling learners.[12] For the Cornell method, students will fold their note paper in half and on one half ask

---

12. Pauk, H. (2001). *How to Study in College 7th Ed.* Houghton Mifflin Company.

themselves questions. The teacher guides students through this process, perhaps offering questions that might appear on a test. An example would be, "what are the eight planets?" Then on the other half of the note paper the student would write down all eight planets. When it comes to study time, they just fold their paper in half and read the questions. It is almost like making note cards without the note cards. One side is the question the other side is the notes. Some really creative teachers have created origami notes, where you have a question and then you open up the flap and there is the answer. These are just some creative and engaging ways to remember the information because students are taking a lot of notes for a lot of different teachers. The teacher needs to make the subject "come alive" for the students. There are all different types of note taking methods, but teaching the methods to the students, or better yet allowing students to find the ones that work for them will help students develop an important skill that can help them be successful in college or organizing their thoughts for the work world. In addition, effectively taking notes can be a very important skill for students when they attend church to assist them in better understanding content from multiple avenues.

Think, Pair, Share

In this method the teacher provokes students' thinking with a question, prompt or observation. The students should take a few moments (probably not minutes) just to *think* about the question. Using designated partners, nearby neighbors, or a desk mate, students *pair* up to talk about the answer each came up with. They compare their mental or written notes and identify the answers they think are best, most convincing, or most unique. After students talk in pairs for a few moments (again, usually not minutes), the teacher calls for pairs to *share* their thinking with the rest of the class. Teachers can do this by going around the room in round-robin fashion, calling on each pair, or they can take answers as they are called out (or as hands are raised). Often, the teacher or a designated helper will record these responses on the board or on the overhead. In addition to being an engaging activity, this also allows for a quick informal teacher assessment of student understanding of the content/topic.

Collaboration, Independence, Cooperation

There are many different types of learning styles (e.g., kinesthetic, auditory, visual, etc.). However, one thing that is very important to remember in differentiated instruction is that while we are teaching to strengths, we also want to encourage growth in the areas of weaknesses. For example, a student may be an independent learner. All the assessments and observations of the student show the teacher that he or she is an intrapersonal learner and performs best working independently on activities. However, in the future, students will not always get to work independently in life. They will have to work with other people in the work place and other scenarios. Thus, while a student's strength is working independently, and that's how a teacher would want him or her to prepare for tests and assessments, the teacher shouldn't want to completely keep the student away from collaboration and cooperation. This is also very important with the modes of expression. Students may learn through independence, but they must be stretched through collaboration and cooperation to prepare them for their future education and careers. Teachers will need to find the balance of not protecting their students too much from their weaknesses while at the same time keeping students engaged and comfortable and in a safe environment in their learning.

High Preparation Differentiation

The previous ideas are for teachers who are new to differentiated instruction. Once a teacher begins to feel more comfortable and sees the benefits of differentiated instruction, there are many more creative ideas that can be used that require a little more planning. Some of these ideas have either already been discussed, are self-explanatory, or will be discussed later. Other ideas will follow the list.

High Preparation Differentiation[13]

Class-Wide Strategies

- Class-Wide Tutoring
- Multiple Texts
- Independent Studies
- Stations
- Literature Circles
- Interest Circles
- Tape Recorded Materials
- Group Investigation
- Community Mentors

Educating and Assessing for Success

- Learning Strategies
- Tiered Activities/Labs
- Tiered Products
- Tiered Centers
- Learning Contracts
- Multiple Intelligences Options
- Spelling by Readiness
- Teams, Games, Tournaments
- Alternative Assessments
- Tic-Tac-Toe
- Varied Rubrics

Class-Wide Peer Tutoring
Using the buddy system was already discussed, but that is considered a low-preparation example of differentiated instruction and usually refers to informally having one student occasionally help others. A peer tutoring system is something formal that a teacher creates. Students earn this privilege, and they get a badge that designates them for this privilege. The student then has very specific training and tasks involved in being a class-wide tutor. Even high school students who are interested in becoming teachers may get involved assisting teachers in other grades. This is one example of a more formal and planned system.

---

13. Tomlinson, C. A., (2001). *How to differentiate instruction in mixed-ability classrooms (2nd Ed)*. Alexandria, VA: ASCD.

Multiple Texts

Teachers need to have various texts and teachers' guides for their subject areas and classes. Often the various texts can give ideas for differentiated instruction. Various textbook companies also offer high-interest texts that do not require a high reading level for students who are reading below grade level. For example, ninth grade world history teachers can find a textbook that reads at a fifth or fourth grade level. These are called high-low books (high interest, low level). Trade books are often sold this way as well. A teacher could possibly find a rewritten high/low text of *Romeo and Juliet* that reads at a second grade level rather than a high school level. This is also useful for students learning the main points of the reading assignments while getting more information for the text that reads at a higher level.

Independent Studies

Independent studies are often associated with college-level learning; however, with the availability of online learning and resources, this is becoming common for students at all levels. In an independent study, students study with an "expert" in the field, and a big final project is completed with that expert. Perhaps your gifted student could be paired with an engineer in the community to do some type of special assignment. Now this student is in an independent study environment, instead of being bored by lectures and assignments that are not challenging.

Stations

Stations, also known as *learning centers*, are a good way to allow students to review material at a varied pace. Each station has different assignments. For example, students can go to their spelling words station, pull out a file folder with their name on it, and find their spelling words inside. All the students can have a different list or different assignments. Perhaps one station can have the students use a tape recorder to help them learn their spelling words. Then the students go to the next one where they play a game with other students. These are just a couple of examples for spelling stations, but stations can be really powerful techniques for many subjects.

Interest Circles
Interest circles are way to separate students based on interest. To use the example of a budget again, some students may choose the vacation budget circle, while others may choose the car budget circle, or the finding a job and getting an apartment budget circle. Students can choose the one that interests and motivates them.

Group Investigations
Gifted education programs often do group investigations. This is when a group is given a problem or task and their responsibility is to investigate and solve the problem through testing various hypotheses, etc. For example, a teacher can tell students in groups of five that each group needs to find a way to drop an egg from a four-story building while keeping it from breaking. Each group would investigate this, coming up with plans and experimenting with them. Students could come up with ideas such as making a parachute, helium balloons carrying the egg down, or wrapping it in Styrofoam. However, they come up with all of these ideas without any help from the teacher. Then they discuss how science supported their ideas.

Learning Strategies
Students and adults who struggle with learning most commonly find that certain learning strategies are the tools that make them successful in life and college. However, they are often left to teaching themselves these strategies. As teachers we need to teach our students how to develop and use learning strategies that work for them. The following are the most common types of strategies used: graphic organizers, mnemonics, and assistive technology devices.

Graphic Organizers

Graphic organizers are excellent learning strategies.[14] Graphic organizers are a visual and graphic display that depicts the relationship between facts, terms, and/or ideas within a learning task. Graphic organizers are also sometimes referred to as *knowledge maps*, *concept maps*, *story maps*, *cognitive organizers*, *advance organizers*, or *concept diagrams*. There are many different types of graphic organizers; the list below merely represents a few:

14. Ives, B. (2007). "Graphic organizers applied to secondary algebra instruction for student with learning disorders." *Learning Disabilities Research and Practice*, 22(2), 110–118.

• *Venn Diagram — Used to compare and contrast ideas*

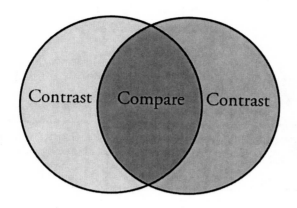

• *Who, What, Where, When, Why — Used for news report stories*

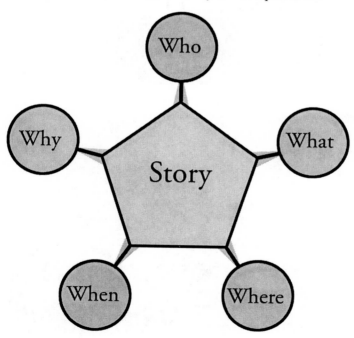

• *Jellyfish*—*used for writing a five paragraph essay. This method can be used to improve essay writing on various writing exams*

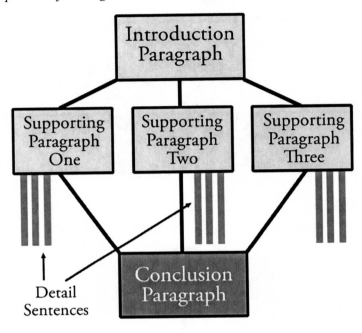

• *Hamburger*—*used for paragraph writing*

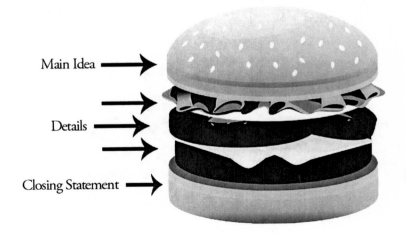

• *KWLs*

A KWL is one of the more widely used graphic organizers for taking notes. The letters stand for: *Know, Want to know, and Learned.* KWLs offer a way for students to build on prior knowledge before beginning a new lesson. Think of the information in students' heads as being files in file cabinets. There are typical learners, who, when told to get out their books, turn to page fifty-six and put their fingers on the letter "T" at the beginning of the first paragraph. Typical learners go through their file cabinets, and in a matter of seconds they have their fingers on the letter "T." The student with a learning disability or who struggles is saying, "Which drawer is that in? My files aren't in alphabetical order." They are digging through files, throwing them out, sifting through information. While all this is happening, the majority of the class is already on the second page. That struggling learner is now thinking, "Oh! The second drawer of the file cabinet," and they are still trying to catch up. The KWL is going to help organize the struggling learner's files. The objective is to get the struggling learner on the same page, in the same file, in the same cabinet. A big part of differentiated instruction is knowing that students need help to get organized. A tool that can help the struggling student is good for helping all of our other students stay organized as well.

Below is the KWL: Example using the Civil War

<u>K</u>	<u>W</u>	<u>L</u>
Know	*Want*	*Learned*
What does the student already know?	What does the student want to know?	What has the student learned?
The students state that they know:	*In discussion, the students ask:*	*After class, a review of what was learned:*
It was between the North and South.	Was it really only about slavery?	That it was about state and federal government rights and control. But much of these "rights" were centered on the issue of slavery.

Learning & Memory Strategies (Mnemonics and Acronyms)

The effectiveness of mnemonics and acronyms is widely supported by research, and most teachers are familiar with a variety of mnemonics and acronyms.[15] Ideally, though, teachers need students to be able to come up with their own mnemonics. Letting them create the sentence or the word helps the student remember and take ownership over something helps students develop the skills that will make them successful in college and life. Below are just a few examples of the many mnemonic and acronym strategies that are commonly used:

- COPS for editing work. Capitalization, Organization, Punctuation, and Spelling

- WRITE. Work from plan to develop a thesis; Remember your goals; Include transition words; Try different sentence types; Exciting, interesting, $100,000 words.

- Every Good Boy Does Fine, FACE, and All Cows Eat Grass are often used in music to teach the scales.

- FOIL for the modes of operation in Algebra (First, Outer, Inner, Last).

Assistive Technology Devices

The existing technology for students can be simply overwhelming. *Assistive technology* is a term that refers to any device used to help students improve their learning. A highlighter can be considered a form of assistive technology. There can be simple tools such as Post-it notes or more expensive tools such as communication devices. What makes a tool assistive is that it is being used to improve learning and that teachers are instructing the students on how to use these devices. Examples of assistive technology are as follows:

• Highlighters	• Tape-Recorded Materials
• Calculators	• Page Followers
• Spell Checkers	• Rulers
• Communication Devices	• Colored Post-it Notes
• Reading Pens	• Varied Colored Writing Utensils

---

15. Fontana, Scruggs, & Mastropieri. (2007). "Mnemonic strategy instruction in inclusive secondary social studies classes." *Remedial and Special Education*, 28(6), 345-5

Educating for Success

This final section focuses on how teachers ensure that students and classrooms are successful when utilizing differentiated instruction. Otherwise, differentiated instruction just becomes another source of anxiety for teachers and students. Below are a few ideas that will help students and teachers be successful in utilizing these delivery methods.

The Issue of Fairness
When the discussion of varying our teaching delivery methods occurs, teachers are often forced to contend with the issue of fairness. How is it fair that someone may have notes taken for them or in a different manner? When we start talking about the struggling learner, it is common to hear from teachers and administrators objections to working with struggling students: "We have three hundred and fifty other students in the building that need our attention," or "I have twenty-four other students in this class. It is not fair for this one student to take too much of my time." However, *all* students should be receiving individualized instruction. And, of course, there are initial fears that go with this idea. "How far should we go? How do we seek to reach each individual student?" And this leads us to the issue of fairness. A great verse for how we handle each student differently is 1 Thessalonians 5:14 "And we urge you, brothers and sisters, warn those who are idle and disruptive, encourage the disheartened, help the weak, be patient with everyone." Some students will need warning, others will need encouragement and help and all of students will need the teacher's patience. Teachers may also hear from students that it doesn't always seem fair. But this is an awesome opportunity to teach students about the varying gifts that make us all one body.

One of the awesome things about differentiated instruction is that *everyone* is taught according to their needs. This helps with the issue of fairness because students are not being singled out. Tiered activities, centers and labs as well as many of the ideas below help educate *all* students for success in a way individual students won't stand out as having special treatment.

Tiered Activities, Centers, and Labs
Tiered assignments involve different levels of activity, student interest, and profiles depending upon the assignment. The important consideration here is that these assignments should include *different* work, not necessarily *less* or *more* work. These assignments are equally active and engaging. An example could be looking at characters in literature. A low-tiered activity would ask the students, "What does the character look like? What does the character say?" A middle-tiered activity would ask, "What does the character mean when he says that?" A high-tiered activity could ask, "What clues does the author give to the nature of this character?" Tiered activities are labeled in reference to the higher order thinking skills found in Bloom's Taxonomy.[16]

Bloom's Order of Thinking Skills

16. Bloom B. S. (1956). *Taxonomy of Educational Objectives, Handbook I: The Cognitive Domain.* New York: David McKay Co Inc.

The Multiple Intelligence Options

Many teachers know about the different modalities of learners (e.g., visual, kinesthetic, and auditory). However, multiple intelligence options take this a bit further. Who are the leaders in the class? Can they lead a group assignment? How about artists? Can they draw or create something rather than write a paper?[17] The following chart helps to explain the various intelligences in more detail:

Ideas for Multiple Intelligence[18]

Intelligence	Ideas for classroom
Linguistic intelligence	Debates and oral presentations, word games and activities, encourage a difficult spelling/definition list
Musical intelligence	Add music to writing, plays. For history and geography use music from the time periods. Lyrics in music that teach a concept
Logical-Mathematical intelligence	Compare/contrast ideas, charts, graphs, timelines. Concrete information with problem-solving skills such as cause and effect
Spatial intelligence	Map, mazes, visual activities through drawing. Drawings to depict time periods, historical concepts, drawing out math problems
Bodily-Kinesthetic intelligence	Hands-on activities, to include role-playing and movement, allow students to move while working on assignments, have activities that require fine motor skills
Interpersonal intelligence	Cooperative learning techniques, group projects, peer teaching, leadership opportunities, observe others and giving feedback to others
Intrapersonal intelligence	Work at own pace, quiet areas in the classroom, set and monitor goals, writing in journals, independent activities

17. Gardner, H. (2004) *Changing minds: The art and science of changing our own and other people's minds.* Boston: Harvard Business School Press, p. 196.

18. Gardner, H. (1999) *Intelligence Reframed. Multiple intelligences for the 21st century,* New York: Basic Books, p. 292

Spelling by Readiness

Spelling by readiness gives the individual student his or her own specific spelling list rather than the entire class learning the same twenty words. It also allows a student to spell things incorrectly in his or her drafts in order for creativity to flow in his or her writing. One thing that is really important to know about spelling by readiness is that teachers should never "publish" or "finalize" a student's product with incorrect spelling. Before they complete that final paper, brochure, or poster board, the student must make all necessary edits to his or her work.

Teams, Games, and Tournaments

Cooperative learning is a high-preparation plan where teachers create teams in their classrooms that are all working toward the same end result or product. For example, each group in the class creates a newspaper on a topic, perhaps an historical newspaper on the Civil War. Points are given to the team based on the grading rubric. Cooperative learning can be used for behavioral purposes and for doing homework, but it can also be used for differentiated instruction. The efficacy of cooperative learning is well supported by research.[19]

There are also some lower preparation teams and tournaments. For example, spelling basketball is a game that can be used in teams for any area. The students pick a three-, two-, or one-point word or problem in spelling or math. This is differentiated instruction as the students get to pick which word is best for them. You can do the same with baseball: Do students want a first base question or a homerun question? They get to pick the question that they feel more comfortable answering.

Tic-Tac-Toe Menus

Tic-Tac-Toe Menus are used so that students are able to choose a variety of delivery methods. However, they have to choose them by creating a Tic-Tac-Toe diagonally, vertically, or horizontally. This gives the teacher some control in putting them in an order that will encourage the choices that meet the goals of the class. There are many examples of these available online.

---

19. Elbaum, Vaughn, Hughes, & Moody, 1999; Stevens, & Slavin, 1991

Example for a Book Report Tic-Tac-Toe:

Draw a picture of the main character	Perform a play that shows the conclusion of a story	Write a song about one of the main events
Write a poem about two main events in the story	Make a poster that shows the order of events in the story	Dress up as your favorite character and perform a speech telling who you are
Create a Venn diagram comparing and contrasting the introduction to the closing	Write two paragraphs about the main character	Write two paragraphs about the setting

Big Powerful Product

A powerful product assignment is just a big project that entails project learning. The classic school examples are the final English paper or the Science Fair assignment. Doing this correctly encompasses everything that has been learned to this point in this book. In addition, teachers and students must think more about these projects; they can be incorporated into all areas of the curriculum on a regular and continuous basis.

Once the teacher has identified what matters in the subject matter, he or she (along with the students) needs to identify one or more formats or "packaging options" for the product. Next, the teacher and students collaboratively determine the expectations of quality of the product. More specifically, the teacher and students would create a rubric. A timeline and scaffolding plan will need to be created so that students can build on their knowledge to the final product. The product must be relevant, measurable and observable. Also, consider tiered activities for the various levels of learners and based on student readiness, interest, and learning profiles. Finally, coach for success and celebrate accomplishments. Reward the students and/or teams by performing their work or having a fair or parent night. Celebrate the joys of learning.

God's Grace and Glory in Instruction

The Bible best summarizes the importance of valuing individuals, regardless of ability, in 1 Corinthians 12:14-27:

> Even so the body is not made up of one part but of many. [15]Now if the foot should say, 'Because I am not a hand, I do not belong to the body,' it would not for that reason stop being part of the body. [16]And if the ear should say, 'Because I am not an eye, I do not belong to the body,' it would not for that reason stop being part of the body. [17]If the whole body were an eye, where would the sense of hearing be? If the whole body were an ear, where would the sense of smell be? [18]But in fact God placed the parts in the body, every one of them, just as he wanted them to be. [19]If they were all one part, where would the body be? [20]As it is, there are many parts, but one body.

> "[21]The eye cannot say to the hand, 'I do not need you!' And the head cannot say to the feet, 'I do not need you!' [22]On the contrary, those parts of the body that seem to be weaker are indispensable, [23]and the parts that we think are less honorable we treat with special honor. And the parts that are unpresentable are treated with special modesty, [24]while our presentable parts need no special treatment. But God has put the body together, giving greater honor to the parts that lacked it, [25]so that there should be no division in the body, but that its parts should have equal concern for each other. [26]If one part suffers, every part suffers with it; if one part is honored, every part rejoices with it. [27]Now you are the body of Christ, and each one of you is a part of it.

As educators, we need to determine what we value in education. What is successful instruction and learning? Is it something that can be demonstrated in a score on a paper/pencil test, or is it something more? Chuck

Schwab is an economic and financial expert who also is dyslexic. He talked about some of his educational experiences in an article in *Fortune* magazine. He helped to put the idea of differentiated instruction into perspective when he stated, "The 'A' students work for the 'B' students. The 'C' students run the businesses. And the 'D' students dedicate the buildings."[20] Differentiated instruction recognizes that success takes on many different forms. How can we spark these forms in our students so they can practice their God given gifts to their fullest capacity to influence the Body of Christ and the world? The answer is simple—differentiating instruction to God's unique gifts.

This book is intended to be a cry out from our struggling Christian students more than anything. This is a call to action from all of our Christian educators and parents to empower *all* students to be part of the body of Christ. Once Christian educators can do this completely, the world will see God's grace and glory through His often hidden treasures and gifts.

About the Author

Dr. Beth Ackerman's passion for children with disabilities is evident in her professional career and studies. Her master's degree is in Special Education from Lynchburg College. She has a postgraduate professional license from the Virginia Department of Education which endorses her to teach elementary education K-8, learning disabilities, emotional disabilities, mental retardation, and administration and supervision K-12. Her doctorate degree is in Administration and Supervision from the University of Virginia.

She taught students with disabilities for three years before becoming a principal for six years at a private day school for students with emotional and behavioral disabilities. She has over a decade of experience in working with children with learning disabilities, mental retardation, and emotional disabilities as a behavior specialist, family support provider, teacher, and administrator. She currently teaches undergraduate and graduate level special education courses and serves as the Associate Dean of the School Education at Liberty University.

To schedule a speaking engagement with Dr. Ackerman you can email her at mackerman@liberty.edu.

See other works by Beth Ackerman here:

http://works.bepress.com/beth_ackerman/

CPSIA information can be obtained
at www.ICGtesting.com
Printed in the USA
LVOW12s2230140716
496396LV00001B/61/P